Developing Num

SOLVING PROBLEMS

ACTIVITIES FOR THE DAILY MATHS LESSON

year
1

Christine Moorcroft

A & C BLACK

AN IMPRINT OF BLOOMSBURY

LONDON   NEW DELHI   NEW YORK   SYDNEY

Contents

Problems involving measures

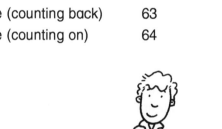

Reprinted 2013
First published 2000 by A & C Black
Bloomsbury Publishing Plc, 50 Bedford Square, London WC1B 3DP
www.bloomsbury.com

ISBN 978-0-7136-5444-8

Copyright text © Christine Moorcroft, 2000
Copyright illustrations © Gaynor Berry, 2000
Copyright cover illustration © Charlotte Hard, 2000
Editors: Lynne Williamson and Marie Lister

The authors and publishers would like to thank the following teachers for their advice in producing this series of books:

Stuart Anslow; Jane Beynon; Cathy Davey; Ann Flint; Shirley Gooch; Barbara Locke; Madeleine Madden; Helen Mason; Fern Oliver; Jo Turpin.

A CIP catalogue record for this book is available from the British Library.

All rights reserved. This book may be photocopied, for use in the school or educational establishment for which it was purchased, but may not be reproduced in any other form or by any means – graphic, electronic or mechanical, including recording, taping or information retrieval systems – without the prior permission in writing of the publishers.

Printed and bound in Great Britain by CPI Group (UK) Ltd, Croydon CR0 4YY

20 19 18 17 16 15 14 13

Introduction

Developing Numeracy: Solving Problems is a series of seven photocopiable activity books designed to be used during the daily maths lesson. They focus on the third strand of the National Numeracy Strategy *Framework for teaching mathematics*. The activities are intended to be used in the time allocated to pupil activities; they aim to reinforce the knowledge, understanding and skills taught during the main part of the lesson and to provide practice and consolidation of the objectives contained in the framework document.

Year 1 supports the teaching of mathematics by providing a series of activities which develop essential skills in solving mathematical problems. On the whole the activities are designed for children to work on independently, although this is not always possible and occasionally some children may need support.

Year 1 encourages children to:
- choose and use appropriate number operations and mental strategies to solve problems;
- solve simple mathematical problems and puzzles;
- recognise and predict from simple patterns and relationships;
- investigate a general statement about familiar numbers or shapes;
- explain their methods and reasoning;
- solve simple problems in areas of 'real life', money and measures;
- recognise coins of different values and find totals and change from up to 20p;
- solve problems by organising and using data.

Extension

Many of the activity sheets end with a challenge (**Now try this!**) which reinforces and extends the children's learning, and provides the teacher with the opportunity for assessment. On occasions you may wish to read out the instructions and explain the activity before the children begin working on it. The children may need to record their answers on a separate piece of paper.

Differentiated activities

For some activities, two differentiated versions are provided which have the same title and are presented on facing pages in the book. On the left is the less challenging activity, indicated by a rocket icon: . The more challenging version is found on the right, indicated by a shooting star: . These activity sheets could be given to different groups within the class, or all the children could complete the first sheet and children requiring further extension could then be given the second sheet.

Organisation

Very little equipment is needed, but it will be useful to have available: coloured pencils, interlocking cubes, counters, scissors, glue, dice, number lines, digit cards, real or plastic coins. You will need to provide packs of playing cards for pages 14 and 15 and small clocks for pages 62–64, if desired.

To help teachers to select appropriate learning experiences for the children, the activities are grouped into sections within each book. However, the activities are not expected to be used in that order unless otherwise stated. The sheets are intended to support, rather than direct, the teacher's planning.

Some activities can be made easier or more challenging by masking and substituting some of the numbers. You may wish to re-use some pages by copying them onto card and laminating them, or by enlarging them onto A3 paper.

Teachers' notes

Brief notes are provided at the foot of each page, giving ideas and suggestions for maximising the effectiveness of the activity sheets. These can be masked before copying.

Structure of the daily maths lesson

The recommended structure of the daily maths lesson for Key Stage 1 is as follows:

Start to lesson, oral work, mental calculation	5–10 minutes
Main teaching and pupil activities (the activities in the **Developing Numeracy** books are designed to be carried out in the time allocated to pupil activities)	about 30 minutes
Plenary (whole-class review and consolidation)	about 10 minutes

4

Whole-class activities

The following activities provide some practical ideas which can be used to introduce or reinforce the main teaching part of the lesson.

Making decisions

Show the sign

For oral work, the children could be given cards bearing + and − signs. Recite a number story, for example: *There were six birds on the bird table. One flew away.* Ask the children to hold up a card to show which operation should be used to solve it.

Number stories

Tell the children to work in pairs and give each pair some laminated 'number' and 'sign' cards. One child uses the cards to make a statement and the other writes a matching number story (or vice versa). The children could also make number statements from stories they read, for example, *The Very Hungry Caterpillar* by Eric Carle (Puffin).

Reasoning about numbers

Partners

Give each child a digit card and call out a number. Ask the children to find a partner with whom they can make that total.

Trio

Play in the same way as 'Partners', but ask the children to find two others with whom they can make the total.

Birthday cards

Give each child a birthday card (either an old one or one made specially) with a large number to indicate an age. Call out a 'difference' (for example, two years) and tell the children to find a partner with whom they can make that difference.

Reasoning about shapes and patterns

Shape feely bags

Put a set of either 2-D or 3-D shapes into an opaque bag. The children feel the shapes inside the bag and draw what they think are in it. After they have finished their drawings, they take the shapes out of the bag and check their drawings against them. Encourage the children to work out how many sides and corners the 2-D shapes have and whether the sides are straight or curved. For 3-D shapes, the children should also try to work out how many faces each shape has.

Postcard treasure hunt

Cut in half a collection of different picture postcards. On the back, label the left-hand halves 'A' and the right-hand halves 'B'. Place a number of 'A' pieces, picture side up, on surfaces around the room. Give each child a 'B' piece and ask them to find the matching half.

Once they have found it, the children take it to the teacher or other adult, and collect another 'B' piece. The winner is the one with the most complete postcards at the end of the game. (Set a time limit, or stop when the pictures are used up.) You could make the game less challenging by using cards which are strikingly different, or more challenging by using cards with more subtle differences.

Problems involving money

Secret coin

Hide a coin in your hand and give the children an example of its equivalence in other coins, for example: *I can change the coin in my hand for five 2p pieces. What is it?* The child who answers correctly chooses another coin and continues. (The same coin can be used as long as different ways of exchanging it are given.)

Money boxes

On the playground or floor of the hall, chalk a number of 2-metre squares to represent money boxes. Inside each money box, chalk an amount of money, for example: 6p, 13p, 20p. Give each child a card showing a coin: 1p, 2p, 5p, 10p or 20p (the cards could be cut to the shapes of the coins). Play some music. When the music stops, the children have to arrange themselves in the money boxes to make the correct amounts. Any children left over are out. The more money boxes there are, the easier the game. As the game progresses, money boxes could be deleted.

This game could be adapted for classroom use by using large sheets of paper to represent the money boxes.

Number stories

- **Write the missing signs. Use** $\boxed{+}$ **,** $\boxed{-}$ **and** $\boxed{=}$ **.**

1 $\boxed{+}$ 3 $\boxed{=}$ 4

3 $\boxed{}$ 5 $\boxed{}$ 8

4 $\boxed{}$ 6 $\boxed{}$ 10

8 $\boxed{}$ 2 $\boxed{}$ 6

10 $\boxed{}$ 3 $\boxed{}$ 7

9 $\boxed{}$ 2 $\boxed{}$ 7

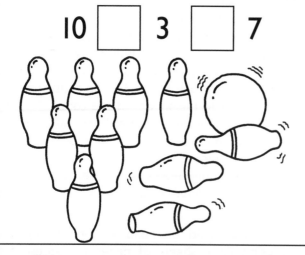

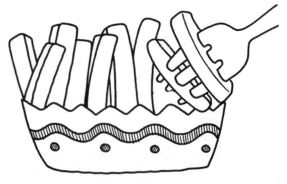

- **Draw and write 4 more number stories.**

Use $\boxed{+}$ **,** $\boxed{-}$ **and** $\boxed{=}$ **.**

Teachers' note You could introduce this activity orally, using the 'Show the sign' exercise on page 5. The activity can be extended by asking the children to arrange sets of numbers and signs (drawn on cards) to make a given answer.

Developing Numeracy
Solving Problems Year 1
© A & C Black

Number stories

• **Write a number sentence about each picture.**

6 − 1 = 5   8 □ 4 □ = 12

___ − □ ___ □ ___   ___ □ ___ □ ___

___ □ ___ □ ___   ___ □ ___ □ ___

• **Draw and write 4 more number stories.**

Use + , − , = **and numbers up to 20.**

Teachers' note Further ideas for practising number stories are provided on page 5. By arranging cards on which are drawn numbers and signs, some children might be able to make up stories involving three numbers and three signs.

**Developing Numeracy
Solving Problems Year 1
© A & C Black**

What will you do?

- **What will you do?**
- **Write the word.**
- **Draw the sign.**

| add + | subtract − |

I have 2 balls.

And I have 2 balls.

| add | + |

There are 3 people in this house.

And 2 in this house.

| | |

I had 4 bones.

I buried one.

| | |

 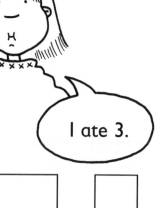

I had 5 sweets.

I ate 3.

| | |

Now try this!

- **Draw pictures and write what you would do.**

| 6 cars in the car park. 2 drive in. |

| 4 cars in the car park. 2 drive out. |

Teachers' note Ask the children to describe each picture and read what the characters are saying. In the first two pictures, draw attention to the word 'and' as it gives them a clue as to what to do. The second two pictures tell a story: ask the children to describe what happened before deciding whether to add or subtract. If necessary, ask, 'Will there be more bones or fewer bones (or sweets)?'

**Developing Numeracy
Solving Problems Year 1
© A & C Black**

What will you use?

- **What will you use?**

- **Join the balloons to the boxes.**

You can use each box as many times as you like.

What is the sum of 4 and 3?

How many more than 3 is 5?

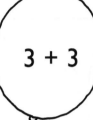
3 + 3

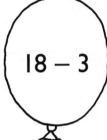
18 − 3

use my fingers	use a number line	use cubes	do it in my head
	3 4 5 6 7 8 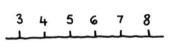	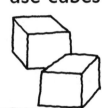	

How many more than 9 is 17?

14 + 5

What is the total of 11 and 6?

2 + 1

Now try this!

- **Write the answers.**

  2 + 4 = _____

  What is 6 more than 5? _____

  What is the sum of 8 and 6? _____

- **Write what you used to help you.**

Teachers' note Once the children have completed the activity, invite them to compare their methods with those of others in their group. Point out that there is no one 'correct' method.

**Developing Numeracy
Solving Problems Year 1
© A & C Black**

Work it out

- ## Work out the answer. Show how you did it.

$4 + 5 = 9$

$4 + 4 = 8$ add 1 more = 9

$6 + 5 =$

- ## Write 3 more examples.
- ## Use the numbers 7 , 8 and 9 .

Teachers' note In this activity, the children can make use of number facts which they know, such as pairs of numbers which add up to 10, 'doubles' and 'one more' or 'one less'. Point out that there is no one 'correct' method.

**Developing Numeracy
Solving Problems Year 1**
© A & C Black

• **Work out the answer. Show how you did it.**

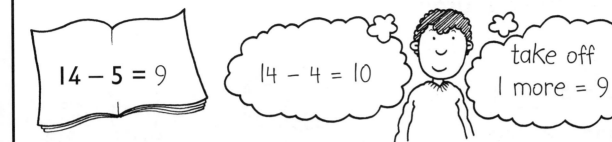

$14 - 5 = 9$

$14 - 4 = 10$

take off
1 more = 9

$25 - 6 =$

• **Write 3 more examples.**

• **Use the numbers** 23 , 26 **and** 28 .

Teachers' note In this activity, the children can make use of number facts which they know, such as 14 – 4 = 10, 23 – 3 = 20, and 'one more' or 'one less'. Point out that there is no one 'correct' method.

**Developing Numeracy
Solving Problems Year 1**
© A & C Black

11

Tell a story

- **Write the missing numbers.**

- **Draw the pictures.**

| 2 + 5 = 7 |

I had __2__ cats.

One cat had __5__ kittens.

That made __7__ altogether.

| 4 + 6 = 10 |

I had ____ conkers.

I won ____ more.

That made ____ altogether.

| 10 − 3 = 7 |

I had ____ pencils.

I lost ____ .

That left ____ pencils.

| 11 − 5 = 6 |

I had ____ marbles.

I lost ____ .

That left ____ marbles.

Teachers' note As an extension, the children could make up more number stories based on operations or number facts in which they need practice.

Developing Numeracy
Solving Problems Year 1
© A & C Black

Flower power

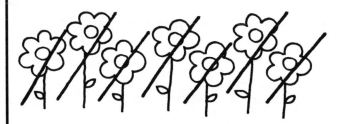   

• **Draw other ways to put 7 flowers in 3 vases.**

   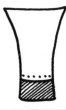

• **Draw ways to put 8 flowers in 3 vases.**

• **Find 3 different ways.**

Teachers' note Ensure that the children realise that they should draw a different combination of flowers each time. They should cross out each flower as they draw it in the vase. After completing the activity, they might be able to suggest ways in which they can arrange other sets of flowers in different numbers of vases, using artificial flowers and real vases.

**Developing Numeracy
Solving Problems Year 1
© A & C Black**

Card totals

• **Colour the pairs of cards with a total of** $\boxed{9}$ **shapes.**

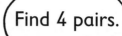
Find 4 pairs.

Now try this!

• **Make pairs of cards with a total of** $\boxed{10}$ **shapes.**

• **Draw 3 different pairs.**

You need a pack of cards.

Teachers' note To make their counting quicker, encourage the children to notice the patterns in which the shapes are arranged. For the extension activity, the picture cards should be removed from the packs of cards. For further practice in making totals, the children could play the activities 'Partners' and 'Trio' (see page 5).

**Developing Numeracy
Solving Problems Year 1
© A & C Black**

Card totals

- **Colour the sets of cards with a total of** $\boxed{16}$ **shapes.**

Find 3 sets.

- **Make sets of cards with a total of** $\boxed{18}$ **shapes.**
- **Draw 3 different sets.**

Now try this!

Put 3 cards in each set.

Teachers' note To make their counting quicker, encourage the children to notice the patterns in which the shapes are arranged. For the extension activity, provide packs of cards with the picture cards removed. As a group activity, you could play a 'totals' game. Give each child a playing card; call out a total and ask each child to work out which other card they need to make that total.

Developing Numeracy
Solving Problems Year 1
© A & C Black

Bags of sweets

- **How many sweets might be in each bag?**

- **Draw the sweets.** 　　 • **Write the numbers.**

Sam has 1 more sweet than Raj.

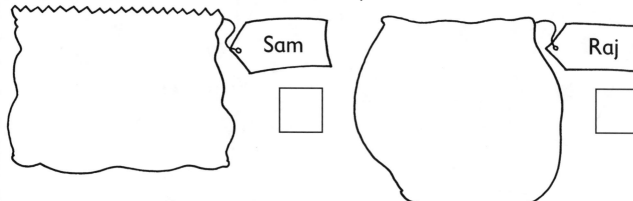

Lisa has 2 more sweets than Tracy.

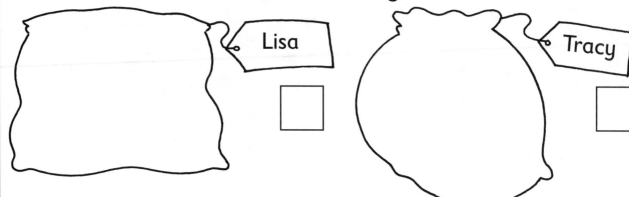

Emily has 3 more sweets than Ross.

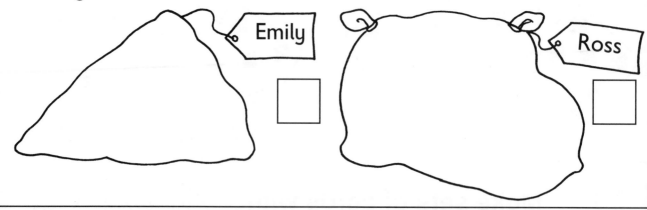

- **Draw 4 different ways of having**

‖ 3 more ‖ **sweets.**

Teachers' note Before beginning this activity, the children might need practice in identifying which of two sets of objects contains more, and by how many. You could use the 'Birthday cards' activity on page 5 to give the children practice in recognising the difference between two numbers.

**Developing Numeracy
Solving Problems Year 1
© A & C Black**

Apple trees

• **Draw** 2 fewer **apples in**

the tree than on the ground.

Example:

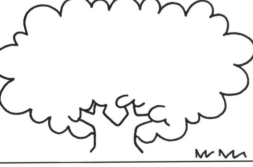

• **Draw** 3 fewer **apples in the tree than on**

the ground. Find 2 different ways.

Teachers' note Before beginning this activity, the children might need practice in identifying which of two sets of objects contains the fewer, and by how much. Revise 'fewer' if necessary.

Developing Numeracy
Solving Problems Year 1
© A & C Black

Balloon puzzle

All the balloons are red or green.

Each pair of balloons is different.

• **Colour and write.**

2 red

_____   _____   _____

_____   _____   _____

These children have 3 balloons.

Each group of balloons is different.

• **Colour and write.**

_____   _____   _____

_____   _____   _____

 **You can choose 2 balloons from blue or yellow ones.**

• **Draw 3 different ways.**

Teachers' note The children could first choose pairs of coloured pencils in two different colours. Explain to the children that a different number of each colour should be chosen each time and point out that red, green, red is the same as green, red, red.

**Developing Numeracy
Solving Problems Year 1**
© A & C Black

Running race

- **Write a number on each runner.**

  Numbers next to each other must have a

  difference $\boxed{\text{greater than 2}}$.

- **Now make the difference** $\boxed{\text{greater than 3}}$.

Now try this!

Teachers' note To encourage greater variety in the way the children arrange the numbers, you could introduce a rule that each number can only be used once. If necessary, revise 'greater than' and 'difference' (see the 'Birthday cards' activity on page 5).

Developing Numeracy
Solving Problems Year 1
© A & C Black

Number triangles

- **Write a number in each circle.**

  Each line of 3 numbers must add up to $\boxed{6}$.

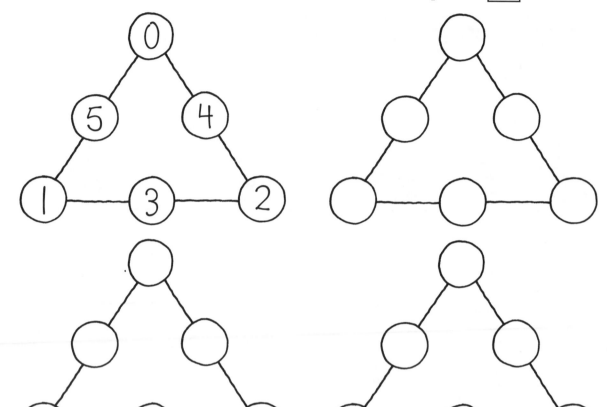

- **Now make each line of 3 numbers add up to $\boxed{7}$.**

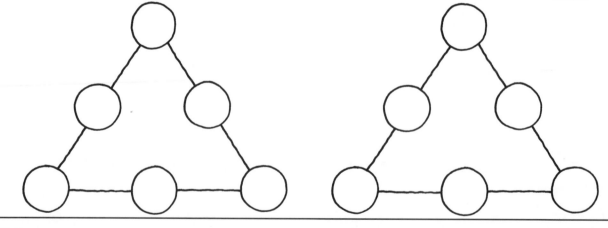

- **Draw 3 other number triangles with lines which add up to $\boxed{7}$.**

Teachers' note Explain to the children that each number triangle should be different and that numbers can be used more than once in a triangle. The children could check a partner's solutions, to see whether any are repeated. They could also do the activity using larger numbers (perhaps working in pairs). Discuss whether it matters in which order they add the numbers.

**Developing Numeracy
Solving Problems Year 1
© A & C Black**

Juggling clowns

• **Write a number on each ball.**

Each clown's balls must

add up to $\boxed{12}$.

Make them all different.

Now try this!

• **Draw 3 clowns. Draw 4 balls for each clown.**

• **Write numbers on the balls. Each clown's**

balls must add up to 12.

Teachers' note To make the activity less challenging, mask one of each clown's balls. Discuss whether it matters in which order the children add the numbers.

**Developing Numeracy
Solving Problems Year 1
© A & C Black**

21

Show-offs

- **Are the show-offs telling the truth?** yes **or** no
- **Write some examples to check.**

I can make 4 by adding two numbers.

yes

Examples

$$2 + 2 = 4$$
$$3 + 1 = 4$$

I can make one by adding two whole numbers.

I can make 3 by doubling a number.

I can make 6 by doubling a number.

- **Write a statement about making** 5 **.**
- **Write examples.**

Teachers' note The children should find as many examples as they can to support each statement. Discuss their answers. Has anyone proved a statement untrue which others thought was true?

Developing Numeracy
Solving Problems Year 1
© A & C Black

Is it true?

- **Is it true?**  ☑ **or** ☒

- **Write some examples to check.**

Examples

I can make 4 by taking a number away from another. ☑

$$5 - 1 = 4$$
$$6 - 2 = 4$$
$$9 - 5 = 4$$

I can make 5 by taking a number away from another. ☐

_____

_____

_____

When I put 5 counters into 2 groups, the groups are different. ☐

When I put 7 counters into 2 groups, the groups are the same. ☐

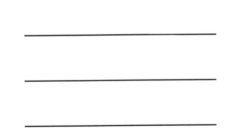

- **Write a statement about making** ☐ 6 ☐ .

- **Write examples.**

Teachers' note If the children have found nothing to disprove a statement, you could display it and challenge the children to disprove it.

Developing Numeracy
Solving Problems Year 1
© A & C Black

23

Check it

- Is it true? ☑ or ☒

- **Write some examples to check.**

Examples

$$\underline{2 + 2 = 4}$$
$$\underline{2 + 6 = 8}$$
$$6 + 10 = 16$$

If you add 2 even numbers, the answer is always even. ✓

If you add 2 odd numbers, the answer is always odd. ☐

If you add an odd number and an even number, the answer is always odd. ☐

If you put 5 sweets into 2 bags, there will be the same number of sweets in each bag. ☐

Now try this!

- **Write a statement about putting 6 seeds into 2 pots.**

Write examples.

Teachers' note This page could be used as an extension of the activities on pages 22 and 23. If necessary, revise 'odd' and 'even'. Encourage the children to make observations about their work in mathematics, for example: draw their attention to the answers when they add an odd and an even number; ask them to make a statement about it and then to check it against other examples.

Developing Numeracy
Solving Problems Year 1
© A & C Black

Dice doubles

- **Look at the score on the dice.**

- **Write the answer in the box.**

Show your workings here.

 Double your score and add 3. `9`	$3 + 3 = 6$ $6 + 3 = 9$
 Add 1 and double your score.	
 Double your score and subtract 1.	
 Double your score and subtract 2.	

- **Write 'dice doubles' questions for these scores.**

- **Give them to a partner to answer.**

Teachers' note Some of the children might be able to compare what happens when they double their score *first* and *then* add a number with what happens when they add a number to their score *first* and *then* double it.

**Developing Numeracy
Solving Problems Year 1**
© A & C Black

Number problems

- **Read the number problems.**

- **Write the answer in the box.**

Show your workings here.

I have 2 conkers in one pocket and 4 in the other.

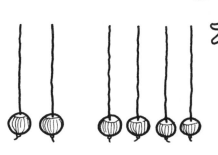

How many conkers altogether?

$2 + 4 =$

Each shoe has 6 lace holes.

How many holes in both shoes?

I planted 8 seeds. Only 3 seeds grew.

How many seeds did not grow?

Now try this!

- **Write another problem about seeds.**

- **Give it to a partner to answer.**

Teachers' note Introduce the activity by giving oral problems to which the children give the answers and then explain their methods (if they need to, they could draw and write on the board or on a large sheet of paper). Ask them first to say which operation they will use. For the shoelace problem, 'doubling' could be used.

Developing Numeracy
Solving Problems Year 1
© A & C Black

26

Number problems

- **Read the number problems.**

- **Write the answer in the box.**

 Show your workings here.

 My shirt has 6 buttons left. 4 have come off.

How many buttons did the shirt have?   6 + 4 =

 We shared the sweets. We ate 2 each.

How many sweets were there?

 I am 6. I am 4 years older than Amy.

How old is Amy?

 Now try this!

- **Write another problem about ages.**

- **Give it to a partner to answer.**

Teachers' note The children could make up 'real-life' examples similar to those on this page, for example: ask them to count the buttons on a shirt and work out how many would be left if two came off.

Developing Numeracy Solving Problems Year 1 © A & C Black

Think of a number

• **Write the number each child is thinking of.**

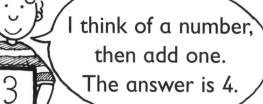

I think of a number, then add one. The answer is 4.

I think of a number, then add 2. The answer is 4.

I think of a number, then take away one. The answer is 2.

I think of a number, then subtract 3. The answer is 2.

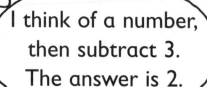

I think of a number, then take away 2. The answer is 2.

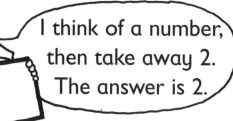

I think of a number, then add 4. The answer is 7.

Now try this!

• **Write another 'think of a number' puzzle.**

• **Give it to a partner to answer.**

Teachers' note This can be played orally, as a game, before the children begin the activity sheet. You could introduce it in a more practical way, for example: put two blocks in a bag and say, 'If I put another block in the bag, there will be three blocks. How many are in the bag now?' Encourage the children to check their answers by reversing the operation.

Developing Numeracy
Solving Problems Year 1
© A & C Black

Think of a number

• **Write the number each child is thinking of.**

I think of a number, then add 5. The answer is 12.

I think of a number, then add 8. The answer is 18.

I think of a number, then subtract 7. The answer is 6.

I think of a number, then take away 6. The answer is 9.

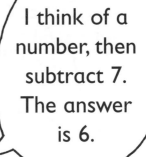

I think of a number, then add 6. The answer is 15.

I think of a number, then subtract 3. The answer is 7.

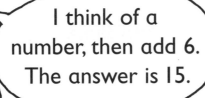

• **Write another 'think of a number' puzzle.**

• **Give it to a partner to answer.**

Now try this!

Teachers' note This can be played orally, as a game, before the children begin the activity sheet. You could introduce it in a more practical way, for example: put two blocks in a bag and say, 'If I put another block in the bag, there will be three blocks. How many are in the bag now?' Encourage the children to check their answers by reversing the operation.

Developing Numeracy Solving Problems Year 1 © A & C Black

Dartboard totals

- **Look at the dartboards.**
- **Answer the questions.**

Show how you worked it out.

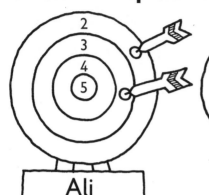
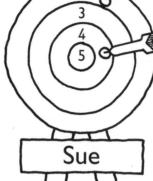

Ali

Sue

Dan

How many do Ali and Sue score altogether? ☐

workings

How many do Sue and Dan score altogether? ☐

workings

How many more than Sue does Dan score? ☐

workings

How many more than Ali does Sue score? ☐

workings

Now try this!

- **Write another question about Ali and Sue's scores.**
- **Give it to a partner to answer.**

Teachers' note Ask the children to identify the operation they will use in each question; they could look for key words and phrases, such as 'altogether' and 'how many more than?' See also note on page 31.

**Developing Numeracy
Solving Problems Year 1
© A & C Black**

Dartboard totals

- **Look at the dartboards.**

- **Answer the questions.**

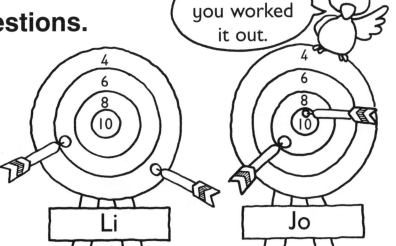

Show how you worked it out.

4	4	4
6	6	6
8	8	8
10	10	10
Ian	Li	Jo

How many do Ian and Jo score altogether? ☐

workings

How many do Ian and Li score altogether? ☐

workings

How many more than Li does Ian score? ☐

workings

How many more than Ian does Jo score? ☐

workings

Now try this!

- **Write another question about Ian and Jo's scores.**

- **Give it to a partner to answer.**

Teachers' note For the extension activity, examples of the kinds of question the children could ask include: 'What did the three children score altogether?', 'Who had the lowest/highest score?' and 'How many more does Jo need to score to make 20?' See also note on page 30.

Developing Numeracy
Solving Problems Year 1
© A & C Black

Bus journeys

- **Write how many people are on the bus at the end of the journey.**

3 people are on the bus.   (Bus Stop 1) 4 people get on.

(Bus Stop 2) 2 people get on.

☐

2 people are on the bus.   (Bus Stop 1) 5 people get on.

(Bus Stop 2) 1 person gets off.

☐

4 people are on the bus.   (Bus Stop 1) 1 person gets off.

(Bus Stop 2) 3 people get off.

☐

6 people are on the bus.   (Bus Stop 1) 4 people get on.

(Bus Stop 2) 8 people get off.

☐

Now try this!

- **Draw and write about another bus journey.**
- **How many are on the bus at the end?**

Teachers' note Ask the children to identify the operation they will use for each step of the problem. They could draw and cross off children on the bus to help them. During the introduction, ask other questions about the bus journeys, for example: 'Can six people get off the bus here?' (i.e. are there at least six people on it?) See also note on page 33.

Developing Numeracy Solving Problems Year 1 © A & C Black

Bus journeys

- **Write how many people are on the bus at the end of the journey.**

---

4 people are on the bus.

(Bus Stop 1) Half of the people get off.

(Bus Stop 2) 1 person gets on.

---

6 people are on the bus.

(Bus Stop 1) Half of the people get off.

(Bus Stop 2) 2 people get on.

---

8 people are on the bus.

(Bus Stop 1) Half of the people get off.

(Bus Stop 2) Half of the people get off.

---

9 people are on the bus.

(Bus Stop 1) 3 people get on.

(Bus Stop 2) Half of the people get off.

Now try this!

- **Draw and write about another bus journey.**
- **How many are on the bus at the end?**

Teachers' note In the extension activity, the children should check their journeys to see if they are possible; they could then give them to a partner to solve. Remind them to use 'half', as in the other journeys. Some of the children might be able to make up bus journeys with four or more steps. See also note on page 32.

**Developing Numeracy
Solving Problems Year 1
© A & C Black**

Piece by piece

- **Cut out the pieces.**
- **Match them to make 2 plates.**

Teachers' note The children could draw patterns on plain (uncoated) paper plates, cut them out and mix up the pieces with those of others in their group. Groups could swap their collections of mixed-up pieces and then sort them out. For further practice in recognising patterns, see the 'Postcard treasure hunt' game on page 5.

Developing Numeracy Solving Problems Year 1 © A & C Black

Matching pairs

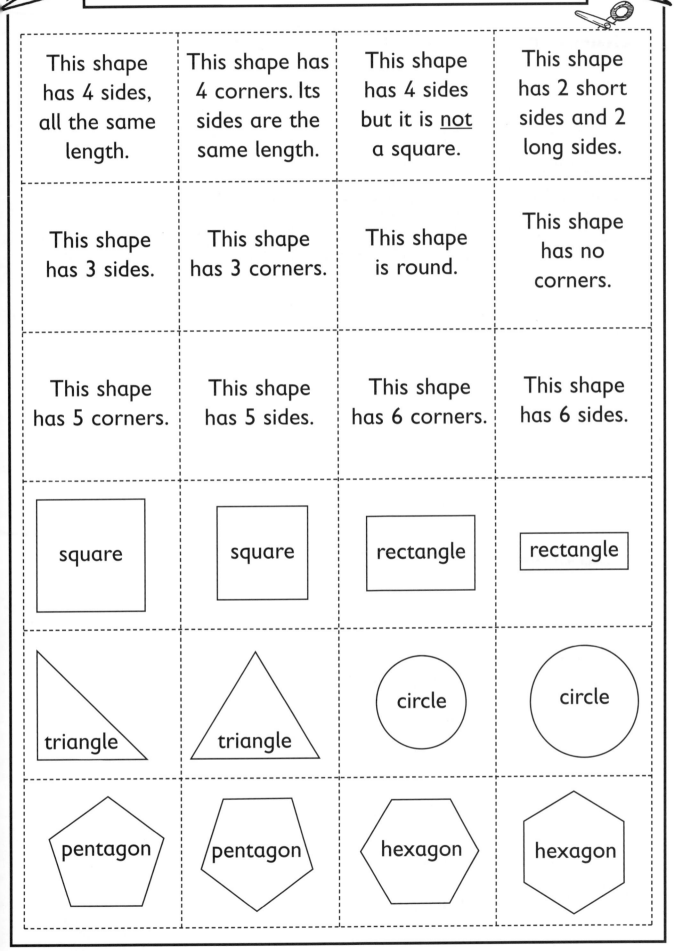

This shape has 4 sides, all the same length.	This shape has 4 corners. Its sides are the same length.	This shape has 4 sides but it is <u>not</u> a square.	This shape has 2 short sides and 2 long sides.
This shape has 3 sides.	This shape has 3 corners.	This shape is round.	This shape has no corners.
This shape has 5 corners.	This shape has 5 sides.	This shape has 6 corners.	This shape has 6 sides.
square	square	rectangle	rectangle
triangle	triangle	circle	circle
pentagon	pentagon	hexagon	hexagon

Teachers' note Mix up the cards and lay them face down in two separate sets: descriptions and shapes. Four children take turns to turn over one card from each set. If the two match, they keep them; if not, they turn them over again. The winner is the one with the most pairs when every card has been taken.

Developing Numeracy
Solving Problems Year 1
© A & C Black

Lie detector quiz

- **Colour the** `true` **or** `false` **button.**
- **Draw some examples to check.**

Examples

A shape with 3 straight sides is a triangle.   `true` `false`

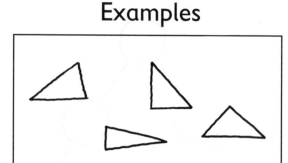

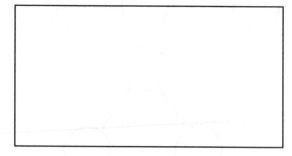

A shape with 4 straight sides is a square.   `true` `false`

A shape with 3 points is a triangle.   `true` `false`

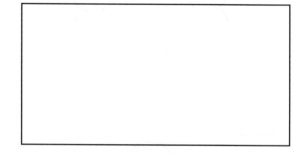

A shape with 4 corners is a rectangle.   `true` `false`

- **Write a statement about shapes with curved sides.**
- **Draw examples.**

Teachers' note The children should draw as many examples as they can to support each statement which they think is true (only one is needed to prove a statement untrue). Ask them to compare their answers. Has anyone proved a statement untrue which others thought was true?

Developing Numeracy Solving Problems Year 1 © A & C Black

Shape puzzle

- **Answer the puzzles. Use the objects in the word-bank.**

Word-bank

ball

book

block

tent

tin

box

It has the same round shape as the sun.

ball

It has 6 square faces like a cube.

_____

It has 6 faces. 2 faces are squares.

_____

2 of its faces are circles.

_____

2 of its faces are triangles.

_____

It has 6 faces. They are all rectangles.

_____

- **Write a puzzle about the shape of this present.**

Teachers' note Introduce the activity by playing 'I spy', in which you describe the shape of an object. Alternatively, you could use the 'Shape feely bags' activity on page 5. If necessary, revise the term 'face'. The activity encourages the children to discriminate between the shapes rather than to name them.

Developing Numeracy
Solving Problems Year 1
© A & C Black

Coin exchange

- **Exchange the coin in the purse for coins in the piggy bank.**
- **Colour the coins you use.**

Teachers' note Ensure that the children understand what it means to exchange a coin. You could use the 'Secret coin' activity on page 5 to introduce this. For some questions, there is more than one possible answer. Ask the children to show how they counted the coins. With which one did they begin and why? (They might find it easiest to begin with the coin of the greatest value.)

**Developing Numeracy
Solving Problems Year 1
© A & C Black**

Coin exchange

- **Exchange the coin in the purse for coins in the piggy bank.**
- **Colour the coins you use.**

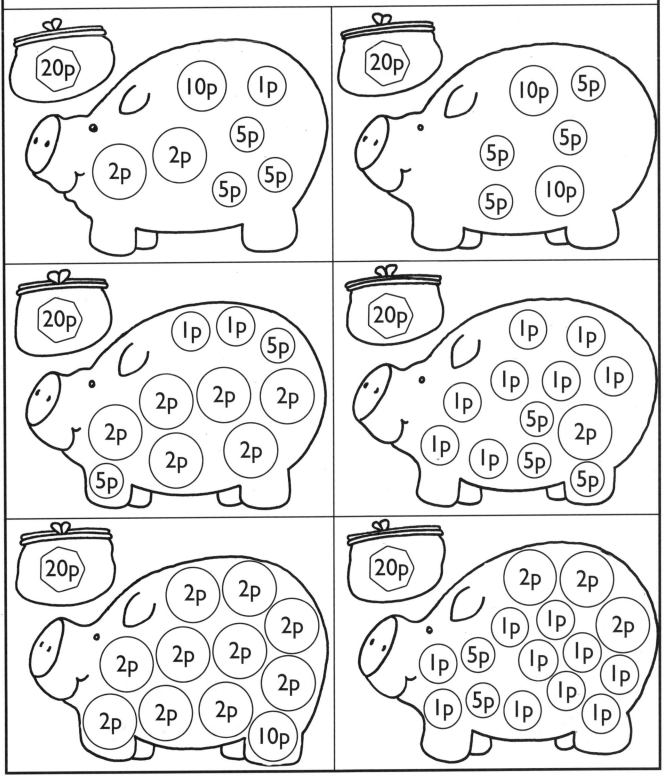

Teachers' note Ensure that the children understand what it means to exchange a coin. You could use the 'Secret coin' activity on page 5 to introduce this. For some questions, there is more than one possible answer. Ask the children to show how they counted the coins. With which one did they begin and why? (They might find it easiest to begin with the coin of the greatest value.)

**Developing Numeracy
Solving Problems Year 1
© A & C Black**

Purse puzzles

- **Is it true?** ✓ or ✗

- **Write and draw some examples to check.**

Examples

I have three 2p coins and a 1p coin. I can make any amount from 1p to 7p. ☐

1p 1p   2p 2p   3p 2p 1p

I have a 5p coin and four 1p coins. I can make any amount from 1p to 8p. ☐

I cannot make 5p without a 1p coin. ☐

I have four 2p coins. I can make any amount from 2p to 6p. ☐

Now try this!

- **Write a statement about making** 9p **.**
- **Write and draw some examples.**

Teachers' note The children should draw and label at least three examples to support each statement which they think is true. Ask them to compare their answers. Has anyone proved a statement untrue which others thought was true?

Developing Numeracy Solving Problems Year 1 © A & C Black

The king's counting house

• **Write how much money the king has.**

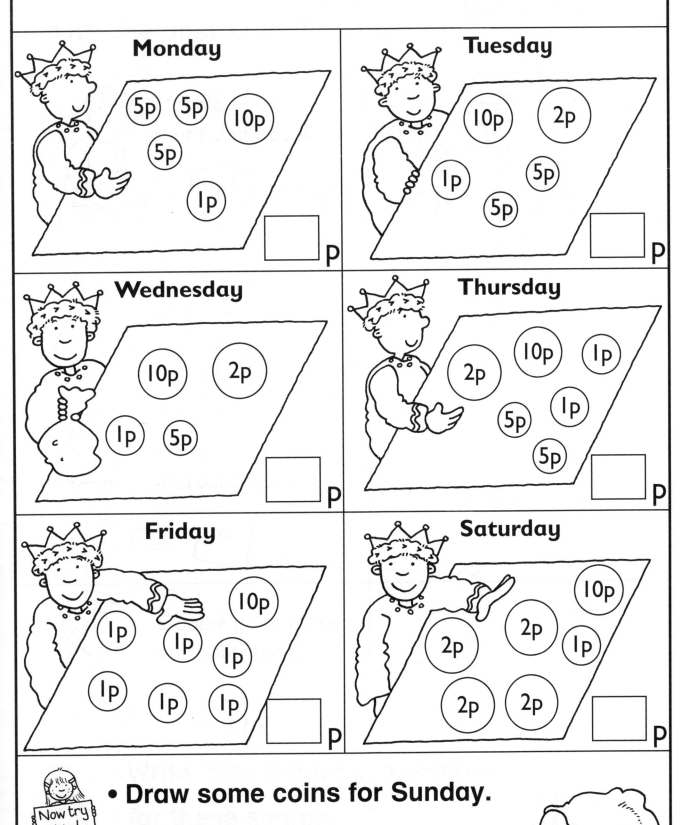

Monday
5p 5p 10p
5p
1p
☐ P

Tuesday
10p 2p
1p 5p
5p
☐ P

Wednesday
10p 2p
1p 5p
☐ P

Thursday
2p 10p 1p
5p 1p
5p
☐ P

Friday
10p
1p 1p 1p
1p 1p 1p
☐ P

Saturday
10p
2p 1p
2p
2p 2p
☐ P

Now try this!

• **Draw some coins for Sunday.**

• **Write how much.**

Teachers' note Ask the children to explain how they counted the money. With which coin did they begin and why? (They might find it easiest to begin with the coin of the greatest value.) How did they ensure that they did not miss out a coin or count any of them twice?

**Developing Numeracy
Solving Problems Year 1**
© A & C Black

Money spiders

• **Write the totals on the webs.**

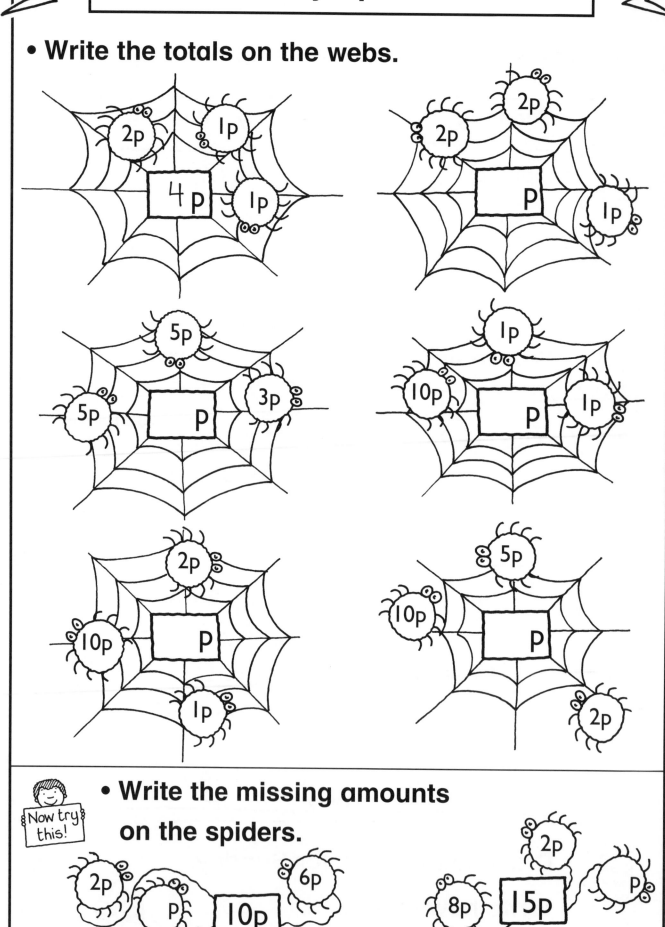

Teachers' note Ask the children to explain how they worked out the totals, for example, they can use 'doubles' ('double 5 = 10'). The children could practise making totals by playing the 'Money boxes' game on page 5.

**Developing Numeracy
Solving Problems Year 1
© A & C Black**

At the tuck shop

- **Follow the lines to find what each child buys.**
- **Write their change in the box.**

8 P

toffee 2p

4p

P

10p

P

6p

5p

P

2p

1p

P

10p

10p

P

Choco bar 7p

3p

10p

P

1p

Fizz 4p

P

FRUIT SNACK 6p

Crisps 4p

10p

10p

Now try this!

- **How much change will there be from** 20p **?**

6p + 4p + 2p = ☐ p   change = ☐ p

10p + 5p + 4p = ☐ p   change = ☐ p

Teachers' note To make this activity more demanding, substitute 20p coins for the 10p coins.

Developing Numeracy
Solving Problems Year 1
© A & C Black

43

Happy shoppers

Each child has 10p.

• **Write the missing prices.**

Ian buys a 🍭.
He gets 2p change.

A 🍭 costs 8 p.

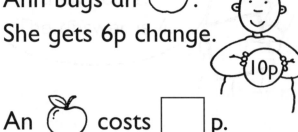

Ann buys an 🍎.
She gets 6p change.

An 🍎 costs ☐ p.

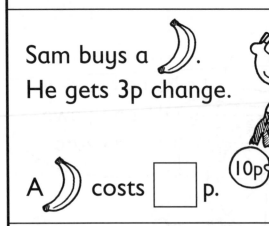

Sam buys a 🍌.
He gets 3p change.

A 🍌 costs ☐ p.

Alia buys some 🍟.
She gets 4p change.

🍟 cost ☐ p.

Ella buys some CHOC.
She gets 1p change.

CHOC costs ☐ p.

Tom buys a comic.
He gets 5p change.

A comic costs ☐ p.

Now try this!

• **If each child had 20p , what change would they get?**

Example: Ian gets 12p change.

Teachers' note The children could make up their own examples using coins and empty sweet packets onto which price cards have been fixed.

Developing Numeracy
Solving Problems Year 1
© A & C Black

Matching game: shopping

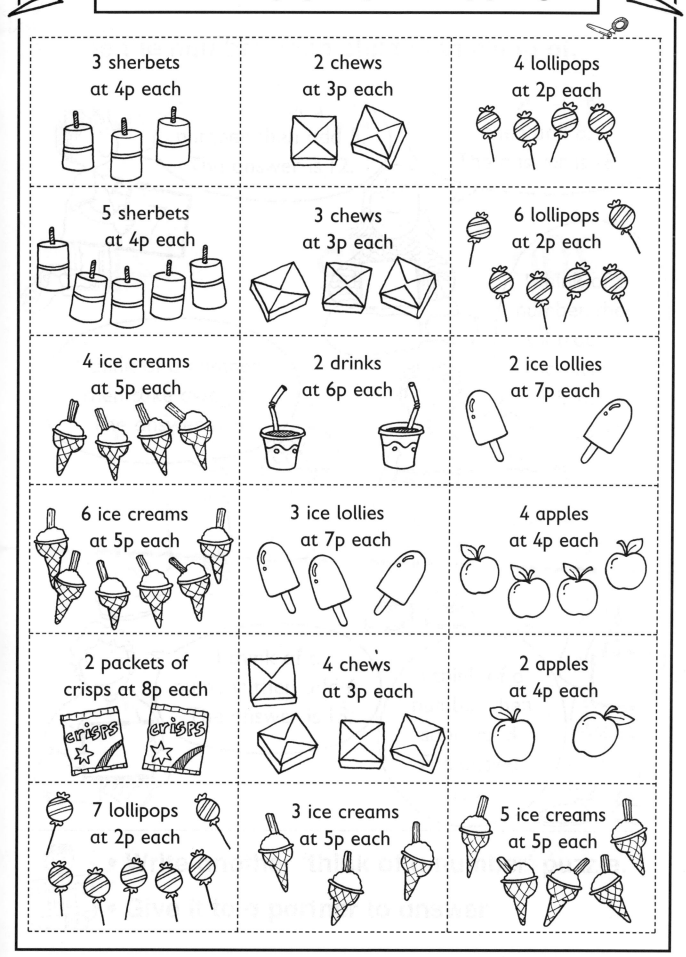

3 sherbets
at 4p each

2 chews
at 3p each

4 lollipops
at 2p each

5 sherbets
at 4p each

3 chews
at 3p each

6 lollipops
at 2p each

4 ice creams
at 5p each

2 drinks
at 6p each

2 ice lollies
at 7p each

6 ice creams
at 5p each

3 ice lollies
at 7p each

4 apples
at 4p each

2 packets of
crisps at 8p each

4 chews
at 3p each

2 apples
at 4p each

7 lollipops
at 2p each

3 ice creams
at 5p each

5 ice creams
at 5p each

Teachers' note Use this with the money cards on page 46. Spread the cards face down in two sets
– shopping and money. The children take turns to pick one card from each set. If the money card
shows the correct total for the shopping, they keep both. The winner is the one with the most
cards. If desired, the children could write the answers on the cards without cutting them out.

**Developing Numeracy
Solving Problems Year 1
© A & C Black**

45

Matching game: money

12p	6p	8p
20p	9p	12p
20p	12p	14p
30p	21p	16p
16p	12p	8p
14p	15p	25p

Teachers' note Use this with the shopping cards on page 45, as described in the notes for that page. Alternatively, the children can simply work in pairs, matching the money cards to the shopping cards. Use as few or as many cards as are appropriate for the children's ability. See also note on page 47.

Developing Numeracy
Solving Problems Year 1
© A & C Black

Coin dice game: 1

- **Cut along these lines.** ─────
- **Fold along these lines.** ─ ─ ─ ─ ─
- **Glue the tabs to make the dice.**

Teachers' note Use this with page 48. The children could also use the dice with the money cards on page 46; they take turns to roll the dice once, twice or three times and add up the amount. If they can, they take a money card which equals that sum. The winner is the one with the most cards when all the cards are taken.

Developing Numeracy Solving Problems Year 1 © A & C Black

- **Take turns to roll the coin dice 3 times.**

- **Write your scores.**

- **Find the total.**

Game I

Name	Scores			Total

Game 2

Name	Scores			Total

Who had the most money in Game I? _____

Who had the most money in Game 2? _____

Now try this!

- **Write 3 more questions about the games.**

- **Write the answers.**

Teachers' note This game is for 2–4 players. First make a coin dice as shown on page 47, or cut out the coins from page 47 and glue them onto a cube. To make the activity easier, delete the third score column and tell the children to roll the dice only twice.

**Developing Numeracy
Solving Problems Year 1
© A & C Black**

At the fair

Each player starts with (10p).

- **Take turns to roll a dice and move your counter.**

- **At 'finish', count your money.**

- **Who has the most?**

start

Play hoopla for 1p.

Your cousin gives you 3p.

Buy a candy floss for 2p.

Buy a drink for 2p.

Your friend gives you 3p.

Win 6p.

Your auntie gives you 4p.

Go on a ride for 5p.

Go on a slide for 2p.

Test your strength for 2p.

Win 4p.

Spend 2p on hook-a-duck.

Go on a ride for 3p.

finish

Teachers' note This game is for two or more players. Each child begins with a 10p coin (real or artificial). Provide a box of 'change'; to pay money, the children need to exchange their 10p coin for coins of a lower value. They exchange money, pay for things and work out change throughout the game. If they have too little money to carry out an activity, they miss that turn.

Developing Numeracy Solving Problems Year 1 © A & C Black

Ticket machines

- **Find 3 different ways to pay for each ticket.**
- **Draw the coins.**

Ticket 6p

(2p) (2p) (2p)

Ticket 8p

Ticket 10p

Now try this!

- **Which of these tickets can you pay for with exactly 2 coins?**
- **Draw the coins.**

3p   7p   9p

Teachers' note The children might be able to think of more than three different ways to pay for each ticket; they could draw extra ones on scrap paper or in a jotter. As a further challenge, some of the children might be able to work out for which ticket there is the greatest number of different ways of paying.

**Developing Numeracy
Solving Problems Year 1
© A & C Black**

Ticket machines

- **Find 3 different ways to pay for each ticket.**
- **Draw the coins.**

Ticket 12p ↓

(5p) (5p) (2p)

Ticket 14p ↓

Ticket 15p ↓

Now try this!

- **Which of these tickets can you pay for with exactly 3 coins?**

- **Draw the coins.**

13p 16p 18p 19p

Teachers' note The children might be able to think of more than three different ways to pay for each ticket; they could draw extra ones on scrap paper or in a jotter. As a further challenge, some of the children might be able to work out for which ticket there is the greatest number of different ways of paying.

Developing Numeracy
Solving Problems Year 1
© A & C Black

Traffic

How can you fit
the traffic along
the roads?

• Draw the boxes and
the traffic inside.

• Write the words.

Example:

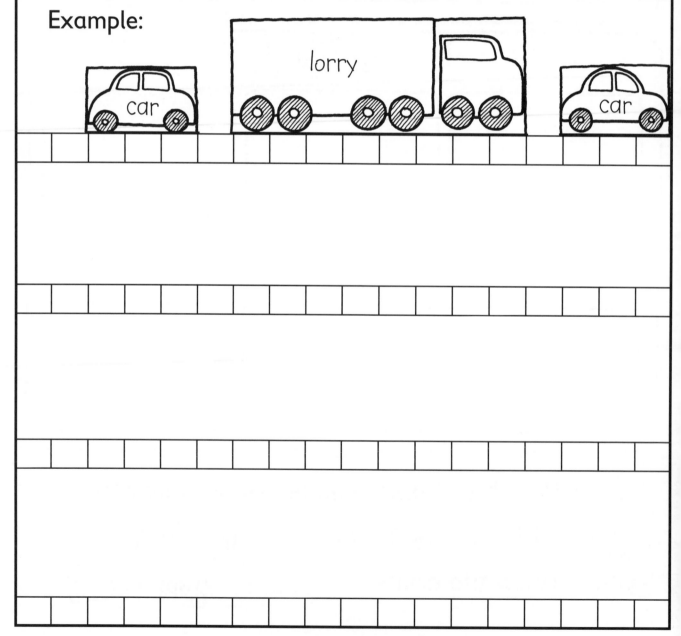

Teachers' note The children could first arrange toy vehicles along a 'road' drawn on paper. The road could be marked in equal segments to allow a space between each vehicle. Before the children begin the sheet, ensure that they realise they can use as many of each vehicle as they wish in any combination, and that they should leave a space between each.

**Developing Numeracy
Solving Problems Year 1
© A & C Black**

Counting strides

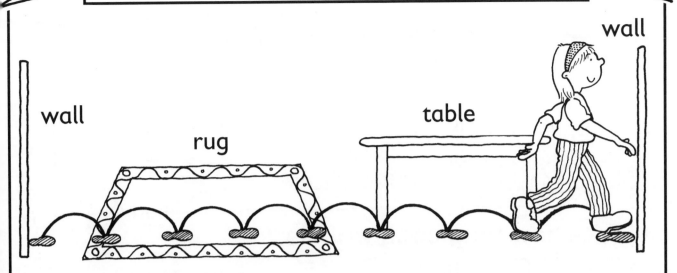

wall

rug

table

wall

Emma walks across the classroom.

• How many strides does she take

to walk across the classroom? 8

to walk across the rug?

to walk past the table?

to walk from the rug to the table?

to walk from the rug to the wall?

to walk across the rug twice?

to walk across the rug three times?

to walk across the classroom twice?

Now try this!

• Write 2 questions about walking in your classroom.

• Give them to a partner to answer.

Teachers' note Ask the children to explain how they worked out the solutions and ensure that they are counting strides (from one footstep to the next) and not the footsteps themselves. Ask them to suggest what else they could do, for example, finding how many rugs can fit across the classroom.

Developing Numeracy
Solving Problems Year 1
© A & C Black

Train carriages

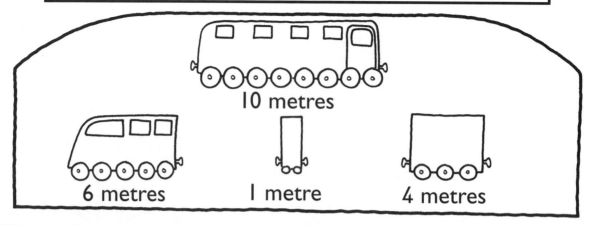

10 metres

6 metres | 1 metre | 4 metres

• Write how long each train is.

6 + 4 +1+1

| 12 | metres

| | metres

| | metres

| | metres

| | metres

Now try this!

• Draw 2 more trains using these parts.

• Write how long they are.

• What is the difference in their lengths?

Teachers' note If necessary, revise 'difference'. Ask the children to suggest what else they could do, for example, they could try to make two trains of equal length using any number of the parts illustrated.

**Developing Numeracy
Solving Problems Year 1
© A & C Black**

Pencil boxes

- **Find a box to fit each pencil.**

- **Fill in the chart.**

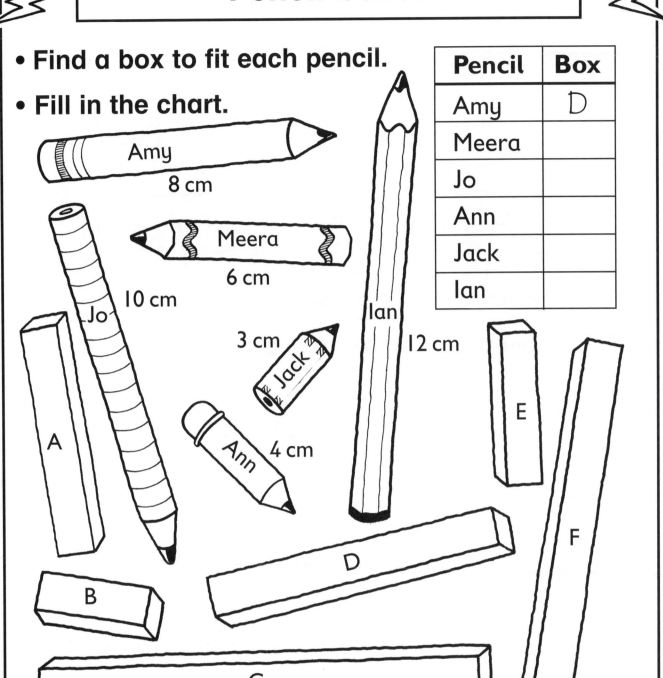

Pencil	Box
Amy	D
Meera	
Jo	
Ann	
Jack	
Ian	

Amy — 8 cm

Meera — 6 cm

Jo — 10 cm

Jack — 3 cm

Ann — 4 cm

Ian — 12 cm

Now try this!

- **Look at the pencils in your group.**

- **Fill in the gaps.**

My pencil is longer than _____'s pencil.

My pencil is shorter than _____'s pencil.

Teachers' note Encourage the children to estimate first, for example, by asking them to look for the largest pencil and the largest box. Then they could measure to check. Ask them to suggest what else they could do, for example: they could work out the combined length of two or three pencils placed end to end, or they could work out the difference in length between pairs of pencils.

**Developing Numeracy
Solving Problems Year 1
© A & C Black**

Make it balance

These scales are balanced.

• **Write how many blocks will balance these fruits.**

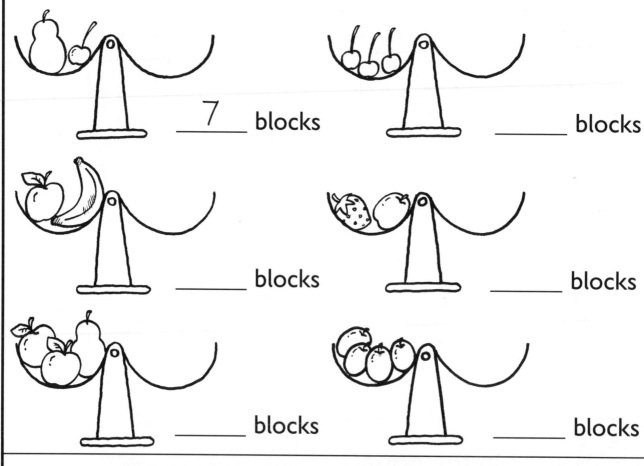

_____7_____ blocks

_____ blocks

_____ blocks

_____ blocks

_____ blocks

_____ blocks

• **Which fruits will balance**

15 blocks? _____

20 blocks? _____

Now try this!

Teachers' note Children requiring extra support could write above each fruit the number of blocks needed to balance it. The children could find other combinations of fruits which balance each other, and write sentences about them, for example: '4 strawberries balance 1 banana' or '1 pear and 1 cherry balance 1 apple and 1 plum'.

**Developing Numeracy
Solving Problems Year 1
© A & C Black**

How much heavier?

These scales are balanced.

• **Write how much heavier.**

___2___ blocks

_____ blocks

_____ blocks

_____ blocks

_____ blocks

_____ blocks

• **How many**  **will balance a** ? _____

• **How many**  **will balance a** **?** _____

Teachers' note This page could be used as an extension of the activity on page 56. The children could work out how many blocks they need to add to a fruit to make it balance another, for example: 'How many blocks must I put with a cherry to make it balance a strawberry?'

Developing Numeracy
Solving Problems Year 1
© A & C Black

Weigh it up

These scales are balanced.

• Write how much heavier.

_____ | block

_____ blocks

_____ blocks

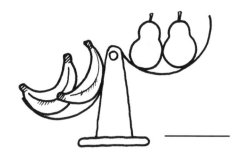

_____ blocks

• Draw 2 more examples.

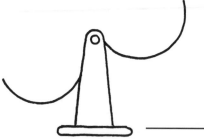

_____ blocks

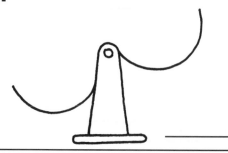

_____ blocks

Now try this!

• Which is heavier?

2 🍌 or 3 🍎 _____

8 🍒 or 3 🍏 _____

Teachers' note This page could be used as an extension of the activities on pages 56 and 57. The children could draw their own combinations of fruits on either side of a balance and decide which side is heavier and by how many blocks. Ask them to explain how they worked it out.

Developing Numeracy Solving Problems Year 1 © A & C Black

Cupfuls

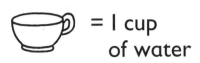 = 1 cup of water

= 5 cups of water

= 2 cups of water

= 6 cups of water

• How many cups of water do these hold?

 ___6___ cups

 _____ cups

 _____ cups

 _____ cups

 _____ cups

 _____ cups

Now try this!

How could you hold ⟨ 10 cups ⟩ of water?
• Draw 3 different ways.

Teachers' note Ask the children to suggest what else they could do, for example: they could work out how many bowls of water are equal to two jugs or how many cups of water would be spilt if they poured a pan of water into a bowl.

**Developing Numeracy
Solving Problems Year 1**
© A & C Black

Tea party

2 cups   3 cups   4 cups   6 cups

• How many cups in these teapots?

___4___ cups

_____ cups

_____ cups

_____ cups

_____ cups

_____ cups

• Draw teapots for these cups.

Now try this!

Developing Numeracy
Solving Problems Year 1
© A & C Black

Teachers' note For the extension activity, the children could first colour each teapot differently, and identify them by colour instead of trying to copy the design and style of each teapot. They could also draw as many different ways as they can to fill ten cups.

Paddling pool

20 buckets fill the paddling pool.

- Read how many bucketfuls are in each pool.

- Write how many more you need to fill it.

 3 bucketfuls — 17

 6 bucketfuls —

 7 bucketfuls —

 9 bucketfuls —

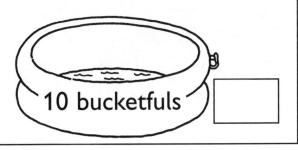 10 bucketfuls —

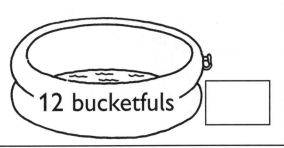 12 bucketfuls —

Now try this!

- Write 4 different ways for Tim and Lara to fill the pool.

Example: 4 bucketfuls + 16 bucketfuls Tim Lara

Teachers' note Ask the children to explain how they worked out their solutions. Which operations did they use? This activity could be made simpler by changing the capacity of the paddling pool to ten bucketfuls.

Developing Numeracy
Solving Problems Year 1
© A & C Black

Let's go for a walk

• **Write how long each walk takes.**

start	finish
3 o'clock	4 o'clock

☐ 1 hour

start	finish
2 o'clock	4 o'clock

☐ hours

start	finish
1 o'clock	5 o'clock

☐ hours

start	finish
3 o'clock	6 o'clock

☐ hours

start	finish
7 o'clock	12 o'clock

☐ hours

start	finish
11 o'clock	1 o'clock

☐ hours

• **Write some** ☐ start **and** ☐ finish **times.**

Now try this!

start		finish
☐	– 2 hours →	☐
☐	– 2 hours →	☐

Teachers' note For question six, it may be necessary to first discuss the change from twelve o'clock to one o'clock. Ask the children to work out the finishing time of each walk if it started an hour later. Some of the children might be able to work out time problems involving half-hours. Ask them to imagine that each walk ended half an hour later.

**Developing Numeracy
Solving Problems Year 1
© A & C Black**

What time?

• What time was it

I hour ago?

I o'clock

2 hours ago?

_____

3 hours ago?

_____

4 hours ago?

_____

9 hours ago?

_____

6 hours ago?

_____

Now try this!

• It is 8 o'clock. What time was it

2 hours ago? _____

4 hours ago? _____

Teachers' note Using clock faces, some of the children might be able to work out times involving half-hours, for example: 'It is half past six. What time was it an hour ago?'

**Developing Numeracy
Solving Problems Year 1
© A & C Black**

Time quiz

It is 10 o'clock.

• **Look at the timetable.**

Timetable

Start school   9 o'clock

Lunch   12 o'clock

What time will it be in 1 hour?

How many hours until lunchtime?

11 o'clock _____   _____ hours

How long ago did school begin?

I had breakfast at 8 o'clock. How long ago was that?

_____   _____

What time will it be in 2 hours?

What time will it be in 3 hours?

_____   _____

• **Write how long it is between each meal.**

Now try this!

8 o'clock   12 o'clock   6 o'clock

      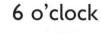

breakfast   lunch   dinner

Teachers' note If necessary, discuss the change from twelve o'clock to one o'clock. You could give the children a list of activities for a story character, for example: 'Little Red Riding Hood got up at eight o'clock. She set off for her grandmother's house at nine o'clock...' The children could draw a time line of the character's day, working out how long it is from one event to another.

**Developing Numeracy
Solving Problems Year 1
© A & C Black**